FRAGMENTS
FROM THE BIOGRAPHY
OF NEMESIS

FRAGMENTS FROM THE BIOGRAPHY OF NEMESIS

Poems

Lois Marie Harrod

Cherry Grove Collections

Cover image: Carole Feuerman, *Zeus and Hera II,* 2004,
        bronze, aluminum, 40 x 36 x 7 inches, Courtesy of The
        Sculpture Foundation, Inc. Gift of Dr. Craig Feuerman,
        on view at Grounds For Sculpture, Hamilton,
        NJ, www.groundsforsculpture.org, © Carole Feuerman.
        Photo: Lois Marie Harrod

Published by Cherry Grove Collections
P.O. Box 541106
Cincinnati, OH 45254-1106

ISBN: 9781625490094
LCCN: 2013930924

Poetry Editor: Kevin Walzer
Business Editor: Lori Jareo

Visit us on the web at www.cherry-grove.com

Acknowledgments

The American Poetry Journal: Headway Beyond Fresh Kills

Bellevue Literary Review: Neither Do They Work Nor Do they Weep

Birmingham Poetry Review: To Walk to Death

Blueline: Catching the Deer, In Context, Pack Rat, The Mist, "Your thorns are the best part of you"

Canary: The Crow, What the Elephant Sings, You Could Buy a New Sky

Center: a Journal of the Literary Arts: Voltages for Different Locations

The Cincinnati Review: Fragments from the Biography of Nemesis

Concrete Wolf: In the Museum of Night

Damselfly Press: We Stay Most When We Stay Not at All

English Journal: Day Lilies, In the Breath of a Fox,

Fourth River: In the Very Distant Universe Objects Older Than Light

Front Range Review: "That Morning There Was Time," We Take a New Road

Glass, A Journal of Poetry: "The Sunlight Has Never Heard of Trees"

The GW Review: Describing Things

The Literary Review: Summer Storm, The Sonnet of Snow

MacGuffin: Walt Whitman's Sermon on Spirituality to a Certain Congregation of Worms

Mandala: Reconciling Rats

The Mom Egg: The Real Spine of the Milky Way

Nashville Review: Photuris Lucicrescens

The New Jersey English Journal: The Litany of Fog

Off the Coast: Six Poison Frogs

Oyez Review: How to Write That Poem That Was Translated from the Bulgarian

Passages North: What the Phoenix Sings to the Ashes

Pedestal: Sex and Hurricanes

Petroglyph: Nesting Song

Pinyon Poetry: Shaft

PMS PoemMemoirStory: Poem with Grave Words

Poems & Plays: Apology, Barn with Snow, In That Long Ovation of Rain

Poetry Sz.blogspot.com: A Small Parenthesis in Eternity

Prairie Wolf Press Review: Sharpness and Sensitivity

Rhino: Firmament

River City: What the Mist Sings

Southern Poetry Review: What the Leaves Say

Specter: Now I Want You Softly

Spire, the Future of Arts and Literature: What the Elephant Sings

Tawdry Bawdry: Truffles Too Have Sex Lives

Terrain: Sea of Appearances, Tsunami

US 1 Worksheets: The Sorrow of Grass, What the Light Sings

Weber: The Contemporary West: Cosmogony, "What will your father say down among the shades?"

Zone 3: What the Polar Bear Sings

Grateful acknowledgment to Finishing Line Press, *Flyway: Journal of Writing and the Environment* and *Poems & Plays* who published a number of these poems in the chapbooks *Firmament, Cosmogony* and *The Only Is.*

I also wish to thank Cool Women and US 1 Collaborative for helpful critiques, the Geraldine R. Dodge Foundation for its support and promotion of poetry, and especially the Virgina Center for the Creative Arts, who provided time and space for me to work on this collection.

for

my husband Lee

my children Jon and Kate

my daughter-in-law Elisabeth

and especially my grandchildren

Will, James, Sophie and Sam

Firmament

Firmament	15
Night	16
Circumference	17
What the Mist Sings	19
Barn with Snow	20
Nesting Song	21
That Dawn	24
Describing Things	25
Catching the Deer	26
In Context	29
What the Leaves Say	31
Day Lilies	32
The Litany of Fog	34
The Mist	35
Shaft	36
In the Breath of a Fox	38
Dream with a Beard and a Gull	39
In the Museum of Night	40
Voltages for Different Locations	41
Slot Canyon	42
In the Very Distant Universe Objects Older Than Light	44
Walt Whitman's Sermon on Spirituality to a Certain Congregation of Worms	46

Fragments from the Biography of Nemesis

Cosmogony	49
Pack Rat	51
Reconciling Rats	53
What the Elephant Sings	55
What the Phoenix Sings to the Ashes	56
What the Polar Bear Sings	57
"The sunlight has never heard of trees"	58

"A Small Parenthesis in Eternity"   59
What the Snow Says This Time   61
Love as Snow   63
The Sonnet of Snow   64
To Walk to Death   65
Anything Goes and Everything Did   67
Six Poison Frogs   69
How to Write That Poem That Was Translated
    from the Bulgarian   70
In That Long Ovation of Rain   71
Poem with Grave Words   72
"That morning there was time"   74
"Your thorns are the best part of you"   75
We Take a New Road   76
Yoke   77
The Sorrow of Grass   78
Summer Storm   79
Neither Do They Work Nor Do They Weep   80
Transformation   81
Pinch   82
"What will your father say down among
    the shades?"   83
"I once loved a poem more than a person"   85
Fragments from the Biography of Nemesis   86

This Pilgrim's Progress

This Pilgrim's Progress   89
Photuris Lucicrescens   91
Sea of Appearances   94
The Litany of the Mussel Shell   95
We Stay Most When We Stay Not at All   96
The Binoculars   98
The Crow   100
You Could Buy a New Sky   102
The Real Spine of the Milky Way   104
Headway beyond Fresh Kills   105
Tsunami   106

Epimetheus 107
How Did Dinosaurs Have Sex? 109
Sex and Hurricanes 111
Truffles Too Have Sex Lives 112
Sharpness and Sensitivity 114
Apology 115
Now I Want You Softly 116
What the Light Sings 117

About the Author 120

Firmament

Consider the cut of cloud,
the lover's hand . . .

Firmament

Great Pond, Wellfleet, Massachusetts

Consider the cut of cloud,
the lover's hand,

the tyrannasaurian claw—
even a child can see

how water catches the heart
and brings it to the surface

like a word rising from a pond,
the great O of existence,

the alpha fish.
We need visible air

to remember what we fear:
yesterday

it was July's dry crab,
today forgetting.

Now I sit in a humid room.
I can feel the wind

binding letters to my lungs.
Firmament—that fragile distance

that should suck us in
and not let go.

Night

St. Johnsbury, Vermont

The horse that explodes light
like an aneurysm in the brain of your sister

or the flash that fills the river
where your father descended below day,

and yet you keep asking
how your brother came to Vermont

when you left him, a dishwasher
at a truck stop, a thousand miles ago.

All day you have been
planning how to elude him,

but now he has stolen
your car and your shins.

That is the way with kin
when they fall ill or die.

If you crawl from the diner now, you can reach
the freeway, flag down a driver

or hide in the roadside ditch
like a handful of peach pits wrapped in his dark.

Circumference

Race Point, Provincetown, Massachusetts

Above the wild sand
the fall guys
stop their careening,
and the clouds
begin to wheel
their jellyfish
into a bluer sea.
The boy who loved me
emptied his shoe
onto the hot shore,
but now I think of the lake
made clear by acid rain,
clearer than the claret
you will round into my hand.
When I was a child
swinging on the gate,
the hinge swung sullen.
Curl your tongue, I say,
it was the same wagon
I spun round and round,
saying anyone can see
the earth is reeling
and the firmament a bowl
of drunken milk.
It was the day
my front teeth came knocking
down the iron church rail,
the night my grandpa said,
why did you do that?
as if I had tried
to spoil my sleep,

as if I had known
what loss was mine
and mine alone.

What the Mist Sings

White Mountains, New Hampshire

The car fades down the follow
where the trees lose

their greens and grays,
your father is leaving forever

as his gods did, that old dizziness
lifting from the far lake,

you looked so gauzy in your dress,
but hush your mother said,

what is whispered clays
the mist, becomes the whitest hair,

do you see your grandmother hazy
on your head and your own face skiffing

towards the groggy urn? The trees
stand close and think

in the vapor of their former selves,
disappearing humps

who can live live now
without choice, without belief

rooted to the spot
as the mist rises

like breath
moving from you.

Barn with Snow

Outside Littleton, New Hampshire

I am so tired of it,
sadness falling like a snow,
the tin roof freezing
beyond the sleet.

Not that I die,
just botch up the calendar
lying diurnal
in the white room.

There are more months
than the narrow moon
you brought on Tuesday,
and all seem sore.

You want to know
why I went angry
to the barn
in the first place,

and I'm not able
to say stop
or to stop miming
forgiveness,

so I turn to the wall
and recant my body
as I've done before
when I'm too cold to sleep.

Nesting Song

Califon, New Jersey

One sorrow nests
within another
like an egg
within a wren,

see her sitting there,
inside the yew
pretending she's
the wooden bird,

her song forgotten.
Think of her grief,
a part of your own.
Think of the triangle

of her bill, the trivial
tongue, think
what gypsy queens
are tissued there:

the girl whose parents
said they spent
far too much
on fencing lessons,

the girl who left
her father angry
with notes about her
leather-jacket friend,

the girl who told
the cashier to fuck off
because the woman
was not polite,

whose house is this?
the girl whose boss
fingered her bra strap
in the video store.

What can be said
can be taken back.
What can be spoken,
can be eaten.

One sorrow nests
within another
like an egg.
The beak opens

and along the horizon
the gray sound of rain.
There are several floods
within each grain of sand.

Be careful when
you empty out your shoe.
Do not suppose
the tongue brings forth

spring's toothless willow.
Cut off its branches,
it grows roots.
Cut out its roots,

it grows branches.
Its leaves are filled
with tents of angry
caterpillars.

The flood, the sluice,
the silky yolk.
Women in cities,
imagine your fingers

around a trowel.
Women on sidewalks,
shower when you return,
watch the taxi careen

down the drain.
It is raining again.
Someone will bring
you flowers the day

you sing deep in the dark cafe,
someone will bring
you freesias,
how sweet of him.

That Dawn

Wellfleet, Massachusetts

When he rose
from the sea
a hungry blossom,

that creature
she had schooled
her knees to love,

her lids lifting
the white caps
against her lashes,

he became a pit,
black and bottomless
as an angel

against the substantial sun,
naked as a maelstrom
in a swirl of sheets.

There were things
she could touch
and things she couldn't,

but which was he?

Descripting Things

"I think I will go on describing things
to make sure they really happened." Stephen Dunn

Sometimes hiking in these New Hampshire hills
I want a Babylonian packet
on which to press my poem,
the soft clay of experience and its sharp stylus,
which is not unlike the pain of a loosening tooth,
that sweet needle at the gum
I can still remember from fifth grade
where the radiator hissed as I tortured
a molar back and forth
wanting the pain to wait my pleasure
because I knew even then
how quickly ache gives way to emptiness.

When I bit the back of my hand,
I could see how small my loss
but when I felt it with my tongue,
it was the gap that kept Lazarus
from dropping water
into the rich man's mouth.

Look how the ledge
gives way.

Catching the Deer

Hopewell, New Jersey

You do not desire
to take the dog early
into this morning
with its thick sky
and dark air,
and you do not know
if the drops fall
from leaves or the clouds
which, as you continue
seem to lift only
to let you see
that they have become
dingy ruffles
worn over a muddy field,
and you want to go home,
wherever it is
home has gone,
and you ask again
what you are doing
so early in the dawn,
but the dog is happy
and suddenly you too
are walking faster,
a note starting
like phlegm in the throat,
you with that awkward voice
your music teacher found hilarious,
and suddenly you step by
the white church
and move into the meadow
where the goldenrod

and asters have worn ragged
in their Sunday clothes,
and you wonder
if it has been
only the poverty
of their undergarments
that they have relinquished
to the skies,
and under it all
the salvation army
is collecting hand-me-downs
and maybe today
you will stop dying,
for suddenly
in the hedge row gap
you see a fawn
and then a stag
watching
like naked angels
and your dog
sees too,
your dog lumbers after
like a song off key,
and they lift across the weeds,
lucid arpeggios,
like wild corn,
like wild grasshoppers
confusing the birds.
And then they are gone
except the stag in the distance
still watching
and your dog
who was never trained to hunt
stands there
his noise stiff in the air,

his right paw raised
pointing towards
what he cannot catch.

In Context

Deer Island, Maine

I am standing on that window sill
from which later in this poem
the Polish poet will leap
and for a moment hold the air
like Icarus and then drop
like a feather brushing the wind,
you know the painting, the boy
floating down to the water
with cerulean plumes as if
he were not falling, the way I would like to die
today or any day, quietly,
with no one noticing
since there is no one to stop the voices
in my ear, but you want to know
what they say.

They say *lead* and *ice*,
nothing that makes much sense
outside the world of gravity.
Of course, there are the lighter
forms, steam and vapor,
and the more solid
hospital bill, thousands of dollars
when he fell. They had to take out a loan
for a funeral, so there's
a cardboard box
in the cellar for me,
I cheat at cards with no guilt,
I gamble my words
to the edge of the sill
and lose, here at the

Starfire Motel where
no room is more than
two stories up. It's not
the circus that gets you,
it's the coupon, two tightropes
for a dollar, one to walk
and one to wrap
around your neck.

What the Leaves Say

Delaware Water Gap

It is not our mouths,
but the wind in them.

Here in the birch, something
to hold your breath.

Do you see how we dip?
We touch and tremble.

The lowest among us catches
the lightest sleep.

Sassafras, hang
your mittens out to dry.

The bark pretends
it cannot hear us.

It is not our mouths,
but the wind that lies.

Day Lilies

Route 31, south of Ringos, New Jersey

Consider the man
who becomes an Adam,

the evening whose toils
bruise the sheets.

There are worse things
than knowing you will die:

the sun spins the shell
that weighs the apostle's head,

the cervix opens a garden,
ovaries like patient pearls.

Rosy June and so humid,
the slit bud sags.

There are four more seeds
or none or three.

Do you follow my drift,
the girl denies she is pregnant,

the guy pretends
he was dancing all night.

If you compare breathing
to pollen,

you suck in the rust
that reaps the raiment.

Tomorrow's skin
shrivels like yesterday's blossom,

the trumpet of morning,
the cornucopia of grief.

The Litany of Fog

Frost Place, New Hampshire

I am the fern
flailing the rain
the blunt voice
of needless grass
the salt marsh
fluting its haze
the gray goose honking
where he flies.

I am the fishmonger
with his lisping eel
the spray cramming
its mouth with sand
the tip of the dock
fading to gray
the harbor smuggling
its boat to sea.

I am the village
unraveling its sheep
and the sweater
smearing its sleeve
the path of plenty
that you reap
the path of penury
you cleave.
O tell me
the wet way home.

The Mist

Franconia, New Hampshire

If metaphor
were sufficient,
I would think of mist today
as a silent woman
wrapping her body
around the noise of trees.

But I want to know
how she mutes
everything,
makes the world
subservient
to self,
that sweet
almost translucent
fog of being.

I want to know
how she lays herself
on thorns and thistles
muck and morass,
that place where
the deer breathed
and breathed no more,
how she pulls down
the firmament
and leaves it
hanging in the air
without a voice.

Shaft

Sourland Mountains, New Jersey

Maybe I do not need to tell you
how the sun becomes water

how light spills
the spaces between leaves.

This morning, a thousand lapses
in the oak

and further down the road
between the stains of trees

light jiggers into shadow
like a tiled serpent

and then pours and tumbles
into swilled pitch.

Some make damnation
of such as these

but maybe you can see too
water becoming wood

planks splicing the interstices of air
fern and furrow.

Can you see the house
I am taking,

the nails I steal
from the insubstantial?

Don't get me wrong,
I do not think this world can save us,

only that these photons have followed
a long narrow passage

to find me here
at this moment

in which my body is becoming
a sieve for the sun.

Now you see
the room in which I am sitting.

The window is open.
The desk, ratted with light.

In the Breath of a Fox

I must trot into the past
as I remember it,

dusk growing like the song
to which I have forgotten words,

the foreground fading as it does during fog
until, if I am to see, I must imagine

the clotted yellow of the poplar,
the dark red of the oak.

No habitation this, just the pale
road leading into mist

and the hills no closer
than their mossy trees.

Dream with a Beard and a Gull

Provincetown, Massachusetts

Last night a beard appeared
like an unexpected rhyme,
half-inch of hair over my fair
face, curly as thyme

or is it parsley, and black
as night the wrong side of star.
This is why men no longer desire
me, I said in my sleep,

my beard, my trite gull feet
slipping into the yin-yang of time.
My chin has gone flabby.
I sit and stare and then rant on,

the face shifts like forgotten fog,
the oncoming cars come on,
I know a woman who cannot
stop being angry at the man

who left 37 years ago.
Move on, move on.

In the Museum of Night

The fox sinks into her den
slackly as the sun,

and the slow loris
closes his pink mouth.

The sky loses its patina
a cliché at a time:

you know what I mean,
better safe than surly.

Even the reeds
are shrouded in condoms

and as for the dusk,
everyone is given a key

to open that court.
I fall forward

but slowly enough
so you can catch me,

we watch the bound fish
turning white as a blind.

Where is my bat-skinned
slipper, you ask.

Scour the tub
or I won't get in.

Voltages for Different Locations

And I began to think of my heart as a ferris wheel
suddenly appearing above balloons and electric bulbs
in that field which, for many years, had yielded
nothing but a rusty shopping cart upended in the weeds,

a wheel that for a dollar I could ride above the burdock
and riffraff, one that would disclose on the horizon
hills nested like green eggs under feathery gills,
one in which I could trust the great bolts and screws

wrenched in a noon by sweat and flapping
shirt, a wheel from which I might drop postcards
to the man who tried to climb to that great height

and thought there is no way down but fall,
where I might sit rocking and tremulous, a minute or two,
and then descend, a little wobbly, clinging to the rod.

Slot Canyon

Gaze at the clouds
and the earth opens

slickrock sandstone sluice
long boulder to the bottom

water maybe, quicksand
and a handful of slimy clay

as you pass, dry water
descending into an icy pool

and you, poor fool, you
forgot your wet suit

while the walls fly up into buttresses
sweeping the ridge

you can't change
your mind now

not in this wholly place
that rappels you

down maybe 400,
600 feet

your black-heeled boots
leave indelible marks on the lace

no denying
you were here

but so much bad information
not enough rope to flee

and danger too
if the brown wall of water

closes the canyon
like a dead man's throat

and yet no accounting
for the earthly beauty

what wind and water
can conceive

as if nature had been given
a certain narrowness of mind

not unlike that of terror
its seething tunnel

the erotic gouge
that devours the sky

In the Very Distant Universe,
Objects Older than Light

headline, *New York Times*, 1/14/2000

I try to imagine an object
farther than light,

a stony owl
beyond the moon,

all the dark matter of my life,
rash and wreck–

how much the black rhino eats
to save himself

and yet every black hole
recedes from him–

bone that precedes skin
and devours it,

the place where the hardwood chair
moved across the deep,

the black rose emptying
the firmament.

A child hits his head
and sees red dwarves

but he can't remember
their heavy feet

and what can I make
that anyone will keep?

An infant with the wrinkled face
of her grandmother?

I believe a skull inside a stone
differs from a skull inside the vase

but I have only one hand
and its dark art

and I want to count the black hair
in the white cat's throat,

every feathery paw
that sprawls the sparrow.

I do not remember
the first time I was kissed.

Someone is walking in the snow
like a crow.

Walt Whitman's Sermon on Spirituality to a Certain Congregation of Worms

Open your mouth to the cease that surrounds,
what has been grief becomes ground.

Consider Adam, how dust befell deliverance,
consider Eve, how labor confines.

Oh ye of little space, through you the dead and lying
enter the living, you the belly, you the beast

to another existence, without you nothing creeps
the face of the earth, without you nothing cheats

that which is *the* only *is.*

Fragments from the Biography of Nemesis

I could die for such thievery,
that nothing that is not . . .

Cosmogony

The Great Barrier Reef

I am thinking how pain
fills a space and then leaves it empty

just as time pockets itself
into the universe,

that little purse of nothing
we steal without knowing,

like boys who leave a woman dead
for twenty-three cents, all she had,

or like gout which fills
the rich leg with wine,

and leaves a skin empty
as a voided shell.

I am thinking of the strange names
we give to money, *dough, bread*–

how much have I eaten,
how much left?

I want to leave a nautilus
with its nowhere

divided into visible cells
chamber before chamber:

a slide show–the coliseum,
the gardens, the little tattoo shop

on the corner. It's this simple–
a white expanse on a blue day

whirling into the next galaxy
with an index to every separate space.

Pack Rat

Poor pinch, I say,
filch everything:
the foil, the felt,
the chicken bone
I carried in my pocket
when I was young,
the one that won
my second wish,
the ferris wheel.

Take the ring, the silk,
the silver seed.
Hide it where
you hide
all that taints
and glitters,
the diamond stud
and desperate fling.

Take it to that nest
you enter
and reenter
with all your trips
and sallies,
packs and fleeces.

Oh, the tongue's
a tacky cheat,
but see
how she feels
her way
through dark passages.

Poor swipe, I say,
how dense, how deep
your take,
that little brood
from whence
you buzz,
that ragged clutch
lined with light
so cagily.

Reconciling Rats

If you want something soft and supple
to lie beside, try a rat.

Just one. The kind sold in stores
with survival names like Noah's Ark

or Animal Haven, the one you could buy
for your python or boa constrictor

if you liked snakes. You do not.
You've been squeezed breathless

and now it's the Year of the Rat. The most
you can muster is a tap on the back.

It's difficult to come back from the dead
at first—all that unwinding the sheet.

Yet it's not quite as bad as you imagined.
The little rodent lifts its eyes

and twitches at you inquisitively.
You ask if it is male or female. Male,

and cheap. The clerk too is young and bright-eyed.
After an hour of delicate pokes,

you think perhaps you can hold him.
Your hands shake.

His paws are delicate. You see
Sanskrit and scalpels on your palms.

He wants to be near you, wriggle
inside your jacket. You feel him fidgeting

into your sweater where your heart
used to be. Where it stopped beating not so long ago.

You realize how it will be now:
a dogged quiver at your core.

What the Elephant Sings

Jaldapara Wildlife Sanctuary, India

I destroy
what sustains—
the grass, the trees—

as you have
taught me,
little man with a mouth.

I have learned
the thirty words
that enslave.

I spread the world
over my body—
the mud, the sea—

my brother lost his trunk.
He kneels to eat,
and soon he starves.

It has been years
since dressed in blue stones
I carried the queen.

What the Phoenix Sings to the Ashes

Pompeii, Italy

Let me tell you
how the world remains:

the tortoise balances
two tomes on his spine–

the book of Seneca
and the book of pins.

If you thumbtack your triptych
to Vesuvius, you can not flee.

Even Pliny explains
the lover's three hesitations:

stay, stay here and you will stay
lineaments cased in gray desire.

Now it is raining.
Now a woman is talking to me–

she will keep her envelope
flecked with ash.

What the Polar Bear Sings

Hudson Bay, Canada

White on white, the slip
of midnight clouds

on midnight snow
the stretch of arctic ice

floe to floe
and the waiting

at the breaks
where the seal rises

to bask and breathe.
I walk miles

for the occasional meal,
the black snout

nudging death,
the long sleep

through summer–
that living off

what I can store
of white despair

while those darker brutes
black and grizzly

wander at the edges
of the light I bear.

"The sunlight has never heard of trees"

A. R. Ammons

So I must ask
as it tangles through the branches
don't you see what you are doing
with your balloon of light?
I must say
be careful in the hawthorne with its prods
be careful in the pine.
What would we do
if it suddenly began
raining stars?

"A Small Parenthesis in Eternity"

Sir Thomas Browne

The morning came
like a faded photograph
sucking the color
out of the trees.
Everything lost its motion
except a woman
moving through the gray.
She remembered
the child in a story
where everything stopped–
the filcher, the raker
the candystick maker
fixed like statues
around the square
so that the child
could slide among them
restoring what
had been lost, the coin
to the old lady's wallet,
the red leaf to the oak,
the forgotten oil to the peppermint.
And the woman wondered
whether such stillness
was a common curse
or a cheaper blessing,
what should she lift
from this moment when
the world's heavy commerce
seemed suspended, no gravity,
the letter unopened
on her desk, the baseball

inches from her son's glove,
her husband's car still
on the road
while the steel whistle
fluted on as if
breath were endless.
Then a raindrop fell
and that was it–
a sycamore shivered,
a mosquito lifted
from his larva,
a window opened,
the woman resumed her life
in a moving world,
no longer able to readjust
where she had been.

What the Snow Says This Time

Hopewell, New Jersey

Pretty unpleasant, you say
on your return from walking
the old dog who barks

through dinner, staccato
and alabaster behind the window,
dust on black piano keys

deep to downy base,
rumble of dumb objects
the radio noise that keeps you

from hearing the white whine
of tinnitus. I imagine
my father's face

in his dark box as if the top
were lifted by a white wind,
snow cracking the coffin.

My father imagined bodies rising
on their bony feet, but we know
the universe is flat as a snowflake

and still expanding:
no resurrection this time,
no telescope tomorrow

to scan the marble static.
And yet in the front window,
wild red poinsettias,

the snows of jesteryear
Yorick's snore and mime.
Hamlet's frozen crown,

the snow coil of serpent,
the Milky Way spinning
her ever expanding tail.

Love as Snow

It must fall
It must cover

briar
and tree

devour
the shrunken pear

hide
the frightened sparrow

remake
the world wild

and shimmering
as it was

before
we came.

The Sonnet of Snow

Your feet which are not beautiful lie on the green bed
of my longing, lie against the arch of my hollowed
throat, how do I pretend desire? Will you pose
in the memory that does not exist, the memory of body,

the body I have not touched? It is winter. You are standing
like an egret in the snow which falls around you
in long white feathers. You are smiling. That is how
you understand me, you with your chill innocence,

but the doves have begun to flutter from your temples,
and there is something in the curve of your forehead
that reminds me of stone. From the doorway I can hear

you saying my name as if you were inviting
a delicate insect with pale gray wings to vespers, come,
come, sit on my tongue, sit beside the vestigial water.

To Walk to Death

after September 11, 2001

I am walking today
to that silent City
where nothing moves.

Or if it does move,
it moves soundlessly.

A tower collapses,
an oak falls
through a telescope.

Hawk, glide by.

My neighbor's daughter Sophie
cradles a pigeon.

A squab, not fully feathered,
its beak hooked, too long.

She wants it to fly.

She tosses it up
and it flutters into
a pile of sallow leaves.

Rustle of a dying room.

Another neighbor wants to give me
the hydrangeas she saved
from my daughter's wedding.

Further a wet leaf
flops against the window.

And I hear a small sound
as if my father could speak.

Anything Goes and Everything Did

Went. Gone. Caput.
Vaudeville skimmed off
into the sunset
with its magic scarves.

At the time it seemed
romantic, but then
the geese departed too
in venereal eights,
crating their honks with them
like carry-off baggage.

And all those frogs
with permeable skin
simply slipped into the pond,
no one knew where.

Anything goes,
and you can't fake it–
not one plush hare
pulled from the hat.

Better not sit in the mud,
you may dissolve.
Even a shower
is dangerous.

I knew a woman
who washed
all her hair down
the drain,
happened in a day.

It's not the apple,
but its perfect skin
that brings you grief.

Of course,
there were glib signs
in the dressing rooms.
No hells. No damns.
Have your silk tights on
always, please.

If you've got to stoop to dirt
you're in the wrong
business.

But I want them back,
the dancing pig,
the spaghetti harp,
the pigeon-toed
ballerina, the plate-spinner,
the flame throwers,
the ventriloquists,
the freaks, the geeks,
the individually trained fleas.

I want them all back,
Enrico Caruso
accompanied on the harp
and ocarina, Houdini
stopping the show
to kiss his anxious wife
goodbye forever
and again.

Six Poison Frogs

The first breathes ochre,
cadmium beats
his heart.

Iridescent iris
wet and shining blind
two bulging eyes.

Too much gold
scolds the crow
three carafes of water.

Blue to royal blue before
the red frog chokes
the night.

Yellow dawns
in pentagons, wickedly
fluorescent.

Slick his sex
transparent—
so much light.

How to Write That Poem That Was Translated from the Bulgarian

Begin without beginning:
Night is a culvert. Was.
Ever shall be.

Don't suggest water. Water ripples.

Allow something to happen
though nothing is:

An owl frets. A refugee
begins to riffle down
the meadow road.

Add a note
of inexhaustible exhaustion:
The refugee cockles down
the meadow road
of endless grief.

Do not explain the endless grief,
or why it dimples so?

There is too much
endless grief.

Think about yourself instead:
Who will you be
in the sunlight?

Say it again: *Night is a culvert.*
Remember that you began
without beginning.

In That Long Ovation of Rain

We came at last to center stage
to the delirious edge where wild roses splashed us
in the spotty light.

And hadn't all our labor and all our love
been for this—the opera
which could endure cold quarters, dry bread,
cigarettes and thieves?

But we had not expected to be summoned so often,
to be forced to come and come again
into the rumbling light,
to bend and smile as if we were just beginning.

The rain would not stop.
Even when the curtains shut the last time
and we descended to our rooms,
we could hear it thundering
in the galleries above.

Poem with Grave Words

"One ought not erect monuments to the righteous, for their words
are their memorials." Maimonides

Remember how the lilac mourns for the stars,
that spring of tribes on the bough,

and how the west makes love
to the murk, shucking its moody bruise.

There are no tombs but words
and like the grass, so many.

Even small mouths can fill a farm house
with clouds of fire worm

and the miracles of web and sprig
along the shy edge of swamp

have thrushed the hermit's throat
as far down as his shoes.

The lanes, the grass, the wheat
with its waving syllables, the apple tree,

the copse that becomes the corpse, the coffin
bearing its withered frieze along the street,

that day and this with its flagging iris,
the widower with his chrysanthemums

couching death in an air, what is there to bury?
We do not need monuments.

Sentence the orb we walk, syntax
the night from rim to rim, let the low breeze

drop into the nether black, let it fall
from us tenderly as a friend.

"That morning there was time"

David Keller

As if we could lie in bed counting
the intervals between wet rubies
dropping from the cardinal's beak

and orchestrate the black note,
the crow entering with his
brash . . . *caw* . . . *caw*

As if we could nod entrance to the wind
brushing the drumlet leaves
into their woody *shush shush*

and then the third wren fluting
two hedgerows down
the mourning doves' vibrato

As if the lilac was waiting the grand finale
to stack his lavender trumpets
into a choker for our throats

And the dandelion, golden teeth
to fall into her white song
of breath and dismay

As if the egg that was and is
could not break, as if the whole cosmos lay
in the curvature of our hands

as if that morning there was time
as if that morning
there was not. . . .

"Your thorns are the best part of you"

Marianne Moore

More than one old woman
soft as a peony
has a mouthful of pins

that jab right through
those tough gloves
you've donned.

The spike in the brain,
the thrust, the saw of sex
the sensual conundrum

readies Judith to
hammer the stud
in Holofernes's brain.

He won't feel
a thing and she
will be remembered.

All this nastiness
of the weak to
what? spike the stronger?

And you still
try to be the nice little girl
with a blunt gibe.

We Take a New Road

And snow clots sassafras
and cherry, and snags
the ironwood elbow.

Spreads the sinew, catches
the woody crotch, snow,
the sleepy sex of trees.

While on the steep it slips
down the rock glaze
blindsides the weeds.

Snow on a new road
transforms nothing we have
known. And now your body
beside my own.

Yoke

And what did I hope for when I hoped, immortality?
That gold coin passed from one hand to the next

then suddenly lost in a drawer, closet, chink, dropped
so that an earthquake later, volcano, hurricane,

it can rise to the surface where gold has no value
or small. When I was thirteen, I hoped fairy tales,

the fish on the table cleaves open, and lying there,
the endless life in its gut. I am a princess, I am a beggar.

When I was 15, I memorized *Thanatopsis*
while I was ironing my father's shirts

because my Latin teacher said everyone should know
that hope by heart: *So live that when thy summons*

comes, you will be starching your father's collars.
Didn't the old book say something like that?

It is always been my hope to cram more things
than possible into the possible, the collar first, the stays, the yoke,

the cuffs, the sleeves, this is how it is done, first things first,
the bed, the lip, the mouth, the rising up, the lying down.

The Sorrow of Grass

The sorrow of grass: it can be cut down and continue.
Fescue and crab re-seed themselves. Keep mowing
and new blades appear with the regularity of wheels.

Each time Dürer dipped his dandelion in ink,
the resurrection floated by. This nail, this spoke,
a copper grief. His horse, the pale handkerchief.

It could swallow the sadness of Nebuchadnezzar,
all the grass between the Tigris and Euphrates
swords, lances, spike, pike, knife.

All day my stomach has been green with it,
my knees stained. I am not the first woman to crawl
through history on hands and knees.

Look, the crippled Christina is still dragging
her withers through Wyeth's hay. She can't hear
the child whistling through the blades.

Though her head, like ours, is turned towards
centuries of wheat. How long will we go on?
Fields diminish in a single heartbeat.

Summer Storm

Cockeysville, Maryland

Green wail of trees, a woman's dress flailing up her
groaning thighs, the old drunk next door knocking up
his dark wife, my mother whispers to my dad, claps her
hands over my ears, don't listen, she says. Cocky

the dog crawls into the bathroom, no window,
and cowers in the tub, I hear him whimpering in my
throat. Mom's sits with me on the gray couch, slowing
alligators between light and heave. I say

the window is our TV screen, now we've got one
too, she laughs until the alligators can't be counted
between the thunder eaves and sudden trunk.
My swing mad-jigs off the limb, mounts

the curb and next door we hear rain coming,
big fat footsteps bashing in, *fee-fi-fo-fum.*

Neither Do They Work Nor Do They Weep

Sweet Air, Maryland

My grandmother had lived so long without
that she gleaned the garlic growing beside the road

and brought it to the kitchen where my mother refused
the smell of parsimony on her meat.

My father tried to talk her into rubbing
just a little thrift into a wooden bowl,

but my mother would not, just as she would not
ride a bike or swim, frightened, I suppose,

of any type of stinginess, the lack of earth or air.
Too much was just enough.

When I allowed my own children to gather wild garlic
to make a frugal soup, the odor hung about the house for days,

and I thought often of my grandmother who skimped her smiles
and now lies stripped below her garlic and penury

and of my mother buried beneath the dandelions,
her lilies of the field, wilted with vinegar and bacon,

and then of my father, who tried, bitter for bitter,
to help them live together without weeping.

Transformation

Walnut Hills Nursing Home

How strangely *when* slips into *then*:
the deer downed on the road flips, brown paper

shadows of tree trunks ladder the path,
rung becomes crevice, be careful

your mother's back, once straight
as exclamation begins its question

marking her spine, what is sense any way
except crooks in the road–

are you holding onto your pursed
lips? it won't be long before the thief

steals your story, turns tale into trot–
wolf in sleep's clothing.

Pinch

It was day, fine and blue
but the sun, finicky

as an old woman
whose rooms fill

with the gray dailies
of desire, box and grit.

A sky that
seemed fine and white

but I knew if you entered,
you would touch

something random
and ready to teeter.

It was your presence
in that light,

the way you could
not pussyfoot

through the clutter,
that made you imagine

none of it was worth
a mote to me.

"What will your father say down among the shades?"

Robert Pinsky, "Poem of Disconnected Parts"

Sometimes he begins a sentence
as if he wants me to guess the end

as he did towards his extremity–
today I will cut . . . and I try to guess

what he had forgotten
school?. . . the grass?. . . my hair?. . .

the small needs of a scholarly parson
who liked his turf as trim as his hair.

Sometimes I want to speak for him,
apologize for the saving fluid

that poisons the soil
in which he grew corn and beans

that formaldehyde that keeps maggots at bay
come, eat . . . I think he would say.

Did he not give
more than he owned?

Sometimes I want to ask him
if he still believes in that merciful rain

that fell on my sister
like stones

but my father isn't saying much
from the durable dark,

not much more than he said
from his dogged glow.

"I once loved a poem more than a person"

J. D. McClatchy

And how could I not love it, the poem knowing,
as I did not, what I desired, the moon
slipping into the magnolia like a mourning
dove, the sun coming down on the sea–

while the man had no tongue and was clumsy
with a stylus. But he persevered, scrawling epigrams
on his gawky clay, bringing cream
and coffee in the morning and soup

when I was sick. His mouth made odd little
movements when I was sullen and his eyes
became green rivers in which I learned
to dip. And I knew then that I deserved

him less than the sad bird and the sun,
my man who had no art to say my name.

Fragments from the Biography of Nemesis

"[Nemesis] leaped ashore, and transformed herself into this wild beast or that, but could not shake Zeus off, because he borrowed the form of even fiercer and swifter beasts." Robert Graves, *The Greek Myths*

What she wants she is: borrowed
form, amphora of red peacock,

boy examining his thighs
in a watery dream, I am my own lover

she says, I could die for such thievery,
that nothing that is not, sleep

and its sweet echo. But she does not.
The vase is filling with moonlight,

the clay hocks what is left,
water. Snitch what you can, she

says, mimic no one but me: she swipes
a sleek bath, slips off hesitation.

Within her some lechy god is plundering
his own epic, floating old similes

on the swillbelly sea. She pours
what is left into his cup.

This Pilgrim's Progress

we walk our daily allegory . . .

This Pilgrim's Progress

Hopewell, New Jersey

When we walk our daily allegory,
down Broad Street past Rose and Chubby's
where the pink-faced Fat Boys fill their bellies
on pancakes and bacon, past the Get Slim
Exercise Gym where the upscale lawyers
cycle Nowhere Fast, past Rhodie
the Boxer doing her Muhammad Ali
hind leg shuffle down the picket fence,
begging her quotidian bone like a communicant
at the sacrament rail, we wave to the fervent—
the joggers, the runners, the bicycling priest
who never misses a day, all those determined to be saved
in a faster heartbeat, and the walkers too
for whom we have special affection.
Less pious, the woman who wears a different jaunty hat
every day, the man who reads his newspaper
and drinks his coffee as he ambles along,
and especially the dogs who would lick our sores
if we had them: Winston the Maltese, Lilac
the yellow retriever, Button, Shelby, Shrug.
And most of this congregation gathers in the park, a few acres
with a stream that runs off sump pumps
and sewage tanks, and there
the birds come too—no, I do not call them angels
for this is an earthly allegory, martins, robins, crows,
bluebirds, jays, catbirds, chickadees, and yes, red-tail hawks,
a peregrine falcon from time to time
sitting on the bridge and the great blue heron,
just one in the little park, occasionally feeding in the stream,
though one day, we saw him,
all of us, walkers and dog-walkers and dogs,

in the briary thicket, as big as a pelican,
caught in the tree, wing pinned by thorns,
and knowing we could not get him out,
we conspired to walk away, some saying
they would call 911 or Audubon.

The next day he was gone.

And we wanted to believe he had saved himself,
once the watchers turned away.

Photuris Lucicrescens

Caravaggio may have used a powder of dried fireflies to create
a photosensitive mixture in his uniquely lit paintings.

In the loitering dusk
the lightning bugs begin
their dart and dwindle
as if small constellations

were taking up galaxies
in our ant-ridden peonies.
See how they swirl through
the waves of grass

to the bird bath
where they descend.
Tonight let us call our *constellatio*
Ulysses and Penelope,

the way it flickers off
like love and returns
as lingering. Of course,
we both know it is the males

who wander, the females
who weave lawnward.
Which is best, you ask,
to roam or to remain?

We talk in the fickle light
of the sister who stayed
when she should have left,
of the irresolute boy

who left our daughter,
so much shimmering into dark,
and then of our stolid selves,
how we have stuck it out.

I know if you left me,
I wouldn't wait twenty summers
for your return though
I can imagine those who do,

how one more day hangs on
to the next until decades
glisten into dawn,
how these pale green stars

keep time quiet
though the glimmer
fades fast from the skin,
the face.

Here is my photo when I was 14,
when I knew a boy
who crushed a hundred fireflies
and smeared them on his thighs.

Sometimes I imagine
him reappearing
in the teasel
down by the fence

though rumor has it
he died of cancer
several years ago,
that kind of lingering.

I learned long ago
not to cup my hands
around the glittering, not
to drown gleam in glass jars.

I think Penelope
was shocked when she saw
Ulysses's quivering torso
strut into her mirror.

She must have said to him
I thought you were dead—no,
I thought you were your mother,
as I keep seeing my mother's face

in photographs of my sisters,
as I suppose
they see their mother
muted in me

though I have always thought
I look like my father,
one like you who did not wander
and did not weep.

Sea of Appearances

for my daughter

You wore polarized sunglasses to protect your eyes,
to see without being seen,
to spot the signatures of snatch tides.
You knew to stay one hundred feet
from piers and jetties and playful men in Speedos,
you knew that permanent rip currents existed along such
    seemings.
You paid close attention to children and old folks,
remembering that even in shallow water a random wave could
    destroy your footing.
And you trained
to swim parallel to shore, to out think the break that could
    spoil you under.
And every weatherman
along the coast said, yes, a good time to go swimming.
And now, the rip tide, moving eight feet a second, cleaving
    you from what you cleaved
to, you, a bit of seaweed flipping in the surf,
and what am I yelling from the shore,
just smile darling,
just grin and bear on out until you find
something to cling to?

All the signs seemed right:
a boy from a temperate marriage,
a boy who wept when he saw you
in your wedding dress. Now he's the lifeguard, the one
    shrugging his shoulders,
walking away.

The Litany of the Mussel Shell

I am black water
pouring into
your hands, black
sunrise in the sink, exquisite Chinese ink,
on rice paper, the sign for fan,
the inky shell, what
spelled
and will be spelled,
the chant of urchins, starfish, voodoo of clams, now slack
and white rack,
light rippling across an old crone's nail,
her faille skirt, black
for granny's funeral,
white for the bride, veil washed often, dimity frayed
to thread, night
tattered to day,
sooty shadows,
Einstein's lily, the lip
of gardenias, the curve of space, stars
begetting lace,
the half-sound *shall*,
the bell, sharp
and flat, salt washed onto the gravelly beach, a bone
stuck in the throat
of the gull, clacking
to the sand crows,
come and eat,
there is none like me,
broken as feather along my bony ridges, broken like teeth,
broken
canyons, broken rivers
that marrow the sea.

We Stay Most When We Stay Not at All

If Vesuvius is cloud-quake
this morning the sky is just one more
great catastrophe I want to save
like the little old lady who saves needles,
thinking pine-sharps can pin
the firmament in place–and you
too far to call to the balcony.

But isn't this our way,
you calling me to see the cerulean warbler,
I arriving late?

Pliny the Younger described the Pompeian sky
as a great umbrella pine
while across the bay his uncle
rowed out to meet the ashes.

It's not enough to say
I want you here.

In the foreground,
wild cherry fall away
from blossom.

Somewhere in the middle distance
tree tops turn gold, the Midas dream.
Back inside my new room,
the shadow of branches
clots the blind.

Who wants to be the old woman
who won't give up anything?

Her house smells of rot and mildew
and yet this morning I do not want to relinquish
one thready snarl floating from the mist.
Maybe I should have been a Hudson River painter.

Then I could place you,
a small figure in the distance,
with a top hat and a stick.

The Binoculars

There they were–when we stopped on the ridge, there–
on a flat table of rock, a pair of binoculars, Zeiss,

not cheap, better than the little Bushnells
I left at home, always the one to remember

birding books and walking stick halfway through the hike.
And the question was whether to leave them

or take them. You argued that the person
who forgot them an hour ago would remember

up the trail and come back, for you are the sort
that never picks anything up, no finders keepers

losers weepers in your morality. No *too bad,*
c'est la vie as our three-year-old granddaughter

walked around saying the year after her father left.
I argued that abandoning them was destroying

precious belongings, and that at the least,
we could turn them in at the ranger station

though I suspected someone there, too much like me,
would quietly claim them as his own. Let's be honest.

If I had been alone, I would have lifted them
as I have glittering objects from time to time, advertised them
   yes–

obscurely, and when no one answered, kept them.
And once, I lost the same silver bracelet I found

in a park in Portland, it hung around my wrist until Houston
and disappeared. Of course, nothing we have is of much
    value:

remember when our house was broken and entered,
all our jewelry riffled through, and the only thing

the thieves found worth taking was our tin can of pennies.
We shouldn't leave the Zeiss here, I said. But we did.

It's the way we often are, uncertain of the right thing to do.
Noli me tangere. By now we had finished our sandwiches

and were ready to move on. They would have been
heavy to carry, I said, and the clouds were growing close.

I think of them sometimes, though, lying on that rock,
at just the angle a mouse might scurry up,

peer through the wrong end,
see everything diminishing.

The Crow

The crow sat leafless
in the silent tree

while others whippoorwilled
and chickadeed

or whet, whet, whetted
the dawn

with their bloody blades
of song

until the mockingbird
like me

began singing
for the absentees

the cats and whistles,
cell phones and bells

car alarms, thistles
sirens and shells.

The mockingbird
my brother

singing for others
what he could not sing for himself.

But the crow sat leafless
in the silent tree

no song for himself
or another,

a homeless bird
his black cloak

hunched around
his thin shoulders

making us all
lonely.

You Could Buy a New Sky

Internet car ad

At the lot where Skies are cheap.
I see a cute little Indigo in the last row

but the salesman tells me
the Azure's bigger, safer.

With two children
you want protection.

So how many clouds per hour
can I count on?–I try to sound

wise to his pitch–how much
thunder under the hood?

He gets out the specs.
One bolt of lightning from this baby

can toast
160,000 slabs of bread.

I don't eat that many carbs,
I say, but it might be handy on long trips.

Oh, especially at night, he says,
when there is no moon.

I am concerned about emissions.
Any of these Skies a hybrid?

He looks confused. You know, I say
a Sky like a nectarine—half peach, half plum.

Oh, you mean the Sunset Sky—
we have lots of those with all the smog.

The Real Spine of the Milky Way

My sister's bed: a gray tornado gathering up to Oz and down
among the dwarfs and ducks. Climb on her little wagon with
the charlatans and quack we go.
She's adding cures, her latest—hand-swirl circles radiating
hurricane-force energy. The cure for Dad's forget, Mom's dental
bill, Rover's sleepless
nights, just off the rant side of the meteor. As for the son-in-law
x-rating it off with the sexy radiologist, he'll never get it up
again, my sister will see to that, a simple matter, she says,
adjusting hormones to the stars, some men are much too fit
to live, soon he'll be sick as dodo, dead
as dick, and meanwhile she's raising
a prayer dome over the rest of us,
protecting us from tsunami,
dam failure and shipwreck off Somalia.
And if that doesn't work, she's tracked
down an orgone box. *Doubt*
is not in her vocabulary,
and she seems heaven-bent on wiping out
the species, one rat after another.
It's happened all before,
she says, *karma,*
and she doesn't mean
Noah's flood,
she means
annihilation
of the whole goddamn
human race,
is there
anything
we've done
that she
should
save?

Headway beyond Fresh Kills

Staten Island, NY, 2001

What was a flagging headway of salty trees
became the open sound of broken towers—
slight flashes, worn reefs–the fusty port unnosed
and sodden to the *if* and *whether,* re-schoonered.

Sinking skiff, as if you rake a book,
slug your *nosce te ipsum* boulders,
and stalk on sly. Unread stick
in the craw, headway, landfill, scratching it,

and there a slow crow bobs about in the feckless
way of carrion, gagging on his chanticleer of days.
What's wrong with his *deep dazzled larynx?*
It's racking the roost of what fattens, soundboard

of raze, the groan before *I AM,* ghost in hand
worth two in the whoosh. You scold the salty cedar
and bludgeon through thread-worn dune churning
grass away from the flesh wilderness of light—

can't steal atonement, not from a fetid earth,
so much waste, lamentation
that is all you sow on earth and all
you need to sow before the dark zilch down.

Tsunami

Where mice are boatmen, Kabir

As a cat, that night, the sea—
    black ribbon water fall,
How small we were, tails rowing
      our bloated bellies in the ink.

Black. Ribbon. Water wheels the bank.
     Our father standing stern, unbowed,
our bellies bloated, soon to sink–
      our mother quaking with the stars.

Father stern and unknowing
     no port to starboard, no stem unbowed.
Our mother still, eyes towed by stars,
       rustle of leaves, shaggy ripples.

No port to starboard, no star to bow,
     how small we were, tails floating
through a stink of leaves, shallow laps–
      as the cat, that night, the sea.

Epimetheus

from the Greek επιμηθεια (*epimetheia*) "hindsight, afterthought." In Greek mythology he was a Titan, the brother of the god of forethought Prometheus.

The thought didn't cross his mind.

As if thought were riddle's chicken
    and his mind a ditch instead of a road.

As if thought and mind could meet at an intersection like two cars, one broad-
    siding the other to the resonance of wrinkling metal.

But as if thought didn't crash
    so there was no 9-1-1,
        no ambulance with its teenage EMTs ready to
    rig and resuscitate.

No jaws of death that did not open before the sedan caught fire,
    before the blonde with every bone shattered was
scorched, no engines
        to douse the fire, no siren, no craning necks,
    no cops, no neighbors,
        no dogs, no buzzards beaking blood.

As if mind were horizontal, a line defining the world
    and
    thought
    vertical.

As if latitude
    and longitude could not   meet.

As if both merely continued on their own arcs into space,
    something that might be explained by Einstein,
        whose thoughts were always crossing
            even though he could not gather them
          into a unified field.

As if the mind were the rock on which thought chained itself,
    a brawny Prometheus ready for the eagle, a burly Jesus
        in the apse of a church, beautiful and beefy,
      a naked thought,
  homoerotic,
                    hanging itself before it could
      be
            nailed down.

Afterwards he wondered why.

How Did Dinosaurs Have Sex?

Like great astrological events
in a sixth-grade dream

Uranus aligns with Jupiter
to spawn meteors and moons.

Or just a cloaca for the necessary
comings-and-goings, a squirt affair–

for dinosaurs, like many birds,
probably did not have penises–

just spurted off in the right direction.
Ah, the problems of ejaculation

when the dominant species weighs tons and tons.
My twelve-year-old son wants to know

if they floated on the lake or lay face to face?
Perhaps on their sides, I say,

so those great protective plates
couldn't come between.

Let's imagine it as the union
of a morbidly obese medieval knight

with a two-ton Valkyrie, and we understand
what chain mail does to intimacy–

the complaint, I explain, of body builders,
so much armor between it and it.

He doesn't blush and I continue
the sex lesson for the day.

Except for the problem of propagation,
the mechanics is not important.

It's the foreplay, the strut and posture
along the Jurassic shore

to secure the dinosaur race
which, alas, didn't make it

as we may not either.
Do be careful.

Sex and Hurricanes

Each devastates or disappoints
in turn.

Never quite what it promises
or premises.

Oh this time it will be good,
x-rated, the perfect storm.

Peaches ripen and fall,
crushed in all the wind,

and sighing, torrents to bend
every breakable limb

and then so much damp
and drown or silt

or nothing, a whimper
fizzle of a drizzle.

Like a man who peters out
before his Viagra kicks in.

In my town a man tried to remove
a parking lot manhole cover

flooded by the storm
and was sucked in.

Nothing could save him.
Hurricanes do that.

Truffles Too Have Sex Lives

The New York Times, March 29, 2010

But not one you want
unless you need the flea-by-night
to propagate,

a truffle fly to throb
her eggy soup into your tuber
and shift around your spores

which strictly speaking
are asexual but come
in twos to insure

the genetic shake-up
that prevents love
becoming bleak and bland.

It can't be done,
some say, without
aphrodisiac

and here, lovers,
whatever your desires,
is the fungal lesson.

Sex is rarely easy,
not even for truffles
who to attract their flies

must mimic
anisole and *veratrole,*
those buggy pheromomes

that lure lovelorn insects
underground to plant their seed
and even *androsterol*

the boar's come-on call
to his lady sow so she
can rough them up a bit,

that's important too
some gourmets think
for the gourmet stew,

a hormone so crazy
the hog may eat them all
ripe and maggoty

and irresistibly fragrant
before you can snatch them
for your private Périgord pie

and goose paté.

Sharpness and Sensitivity

Razor–to the skin
Pun's double–to the brain
Wisdom–to Solomon
Some–men to any–woman

Acrid smoke–to the nose
Vinegar–the velvet bud
Aphid–the yellow rose
Screech–to the child–just hushed

Tightened–gut to ear
Finger to hair–trigger
Flash–to gasoline
Fire to paper

Uncanny to the seer
Body to the ghost
Knowledge to the virgin queen–
Thrust and trust.

Knife to boozy liver–
Slick–to style–
Curt to cancer's wit–
Joy to bile.

The short, the inconsiderate,
the thoughtless gruff,
the curt, the blunt–
to each brief heart.

Apology

Open this sentence carefully
as if it were a gift
from your lover
that creature with timorous paws

or your offspring
with crooked fists

as if you can unknot
the ribbon with the same
brute care
that knotted it

or smooth
the shiny paper
as a crag
smoothes into a sea

as if this little gift
contains some
uselessly enameled trinket
you will keep.

Now I Want You Softly

the way a thief enters in the night,
    sliding open the French doors
        leaving his shoes on the mat,

moving his black pants and black sweater
    down the hall, no more than a shadow
    on the foyer wall

but his socks whispering softly to the floor
    so that I hear him approaching,
        can imagine his hand floating

up the banister and dropping to his side
    at the landing, see him through
        my lashes, standing at the bedroom door

a blacker velvet than the black portal.
    It doesn't matter so much
        any more that he brings

what I want, the wild pleasure of slaking
    what is his, only the sweet joy
        of seeing him

desiring the little trinkets I have left.
    Take, I say, whatever you want,
        whatever you can steal away.

What the Light Sings

Not the song of equality–
for there is always a hand

that stops its passage
and leaves traces upon the road

or a government of barns
that darkens the goldenrod.

Sheep obstruct the grass,
and the crow's wing, the beetle.

Even the clouds
with their flimsy thoughts

throw gray blankets
across village and field

so that the child
perched on the porch asks

where is the sky?
why can't we breathe?

No, not the song of equality
which is the song of rain–

but a song that shimmers,
little coins of light

clinking through the oaks
and jingling to the road,

or wings warbling from branch to branch,
until they find a place to linger.

You see it sometimes
in orchards of pears,

the tilt of dawn
along the trunks

as if they were machines of good fortune
emptying

every quarter you've ever spent
back into your life,

or perhaps less random but just as lucky,
at end of day

in a copse of birch,
the spendthrift dusk.

About the Author

Lois Marie Harrod won the 2012 Tennessee Chapbook Prize (*Poems & Plays*) with her manuscript *The Only Is*. Her 11th book *Brief Term*, poems about teaching, was published by Black Buzzard Press (2011), and her chapbook *Cosmogony* won the 2010 Hazel Lipa Chapbook contest (Iowa State University). Her chapbook *Furniture* won the 2008 Grayson Press Poetry Prize. Previous publications include the chapbook *Firmament* (2007); the chapbook *Put Your Sorry Side Out* (2005); *Spelling the World Backwards* (2000); the chapbook *This Is a Story You Already Know* (1999); *Part of the Deeper Sea* (1997); the chapbook *Green Snake Riding* (1994); *Crazy Alice* (1991); *Every Twinge a Verdict* (1987). She won her third poetry fellowship from the New Jersey Council on the Arts in 2003. Over 600 of her poems have been published online and in print journals including *American Poetry Review, Blueline, The MacGuffin, Salt, The Literary Review, Verse Daily* and *Zone 3*. A Geraldine R. Dodge poet and former high school teacher, she teaches Creative Writing at The College of New Jersey. Read her work on www.loismarieharrod.com.

CPSIA information can be obtained at www.ICGtesting.com
Printed in the USA
BVOW032024290113

311884BV00001B/4/P